Editor: Kirsty Hamilton
Concept design: Kate Buxton
Series design: Jean Scott Moncrieff

British Library Cataloguing in Publication Data
Thomas, Pat, 1959 –
I'm telling the truth : a first look at honesty
1.Honesty – Pictorial works – Juvenile literature
2.Truthfulness and falsehood – pictorial works – Juvenile
literature
I. Title
179.9

Printed in China

ISBN 0340 894504

Hodder Children's Books
A division of Hodder Headline Limited
338, Euston Road,
London NW1 3BH

I'm Telling the Truth

A FIRST LOOK AT HONESTY

PAT THOMAS
ILLUSTRATED BY LESLEY HARKER

Hodder
Children's
Books

a division of Hodder Headline Limited

If someone told you that the sky was yellow or that frogs had wings you would know that they weren't telling the truth.

Most of us know the difference between what
is true and what isn't. And most of us know
how important it is to tell the truth.

There are lots of reasons why people aren't honest. Sometimes it's because they feel ashamed, or they want to impress others.

Some people say things that aren't true to get things that they want but don't really deserve.

What about you?

Can you think of someone you know about – it could be someone in a story or a real person – who isn't honest? What sorts of things happened to them?

Being honest takes
a lot of practice.

It isn't always easy to find a polite way to tell the truth that doesn't hurt other people's feelings.

Remember that the people who love you the most will always be happy that you told them the truth, even if it's not what they hoped you would say.

But sometimes if you can't find something nice
to say, it's best not to say anything at all.

13

Often people tell lies when
they are afraid of getting
into trouble.

But lying only makes you feel bad about yourself.

When you haven't been honest it can make you
feel worried and anxious that someone will find out.

Telling the truth helps you to feel good about yourself.

Learning to be honest helps you feel confident and brave.

And you usually get into less trouble for
telling the truth than you do for lying
– and getting caught.

Sometimes it's not what you say but the way you act that counts.

One good way to be honest is to never take things that don't belong to you.

It's also important to keep your word.

If you say you are going to do something,
make sure you do it.

You can also show how honest you can be by speaking up when you see something wrong…

...and letting others know your true thoughts and feelings.

Even though being honest can be hard sometimes, it is worth it.

Telling the truth lets everyone know what really happened.

It helps us avoid misunderstandings and keeps innocent people from being blamed or punished.

What about you?

Have you ever been blamed for something you didn't do? Was there someone who could have helped you by telling the truth?

People who don't practise
being honest slowly lose
all their friends.

This is because friends need to be
able to trust one another.

Nobody can trust a person
who acts dishonestly or says
things that are not true.

Everyone likes to be around a person who speaks the truth and keeps their word.

When we all practise being honest, the world becomes a fairer and happier place to live in.

HOW TO USE THIS BOOK

Teaching honesty and responsibility takes a considerable amount of time and patience. It isn't anything like teaching children how to tie their shoes, where they pick up the basic concept after a few lessons. Instead we need to look for ways to nurture within our children a desire to do the right thing, to value honesty, to say what's on their minds and to act with integrity and good will.

We teach our children honesty by being honest ourselves. Avoid lying to your child, even about difficult subjects such as illness, death or divorce. It's better to admit that some things are hard to talk about than to try to cover them up. It's also ok to let your children see you struggling with issues of integrity and honesty.

Praise your child when he or she is acting in an honest and responsible way. When you are watching TV or reading books take the opportunity to point out and discuss examples of honest behaviour. Use the "What about you?" prompts in this book to discuss with your child examples of honesty and the consequences of dishonesty.

If your child is telling lies or behaving in a dishonest way, find out why. The major reasons children lie are to escape punishment and to get away with the forbidden. Chances are the harsher your punishing, the more motivated the child will be to avoid owning up when he or she does wrong. Where possible, allow the natural consequences of his actions to unfold for your child. If, for instance, he takes something from a store without paying, have him be the one to return it and confront the store manager.

Schools with honour codes and teachers who talk openly about cheating have lower incidences of academic dishonesty. In class teachers and children can brainstorm all the excuses and rationalisations people give for lying, cheating, and stealing, and then have a discussion about them. How valid are they? What's wrong with each of them? What are the better alternatives?

Children learning about telling the truth often go through a phase of tattling. Busy parents and teachers can find this frustrating. Yet tattling – and the way adults respond to it – begins the process of discrimination and self-sufficiency. Dealt with appropriately adults can empower 'tattling' children to begin to solve their problems themselves without running to an outside authority for every little thing.

BOOKS TO READ

'It Wasn't Me'
Brian Moses, Mike Gordon
(Hodder Wayland, 2004)

'Oh, Bother! Someone's Fibbing!'
Betty Birney (Goldencraft, 1991)

'The Boy Who Cried Wolf'
Tony Ross (Red Fox, 1986)

'Pinocchio'★
Carlo Collodi (Diogenes Verlag AG, 2003)

'Matilda, Who Told Such Dreadful Lies and Was Burned to Death'
Hilaire Belloc, Posy Simmonds (Jonathan Cape Children's Books, 1991)

★ Your school or library may have an abridged version of this classic book that is suitable for young children.

RESOURCES FOR ADULTS

'The Values Book: Teaching Sixteen Basic Values to Young Children'
Pam Schiller, Tamera Bryant (Gryphon House, 1998)

'Teaching Your Children Values' series
Linda and Richard Eyre (Fireside, 1993)

'Telling Isn't Tattling'
Kathryn Hammerseng and Dave Garbot (Parenting Press, 1995)